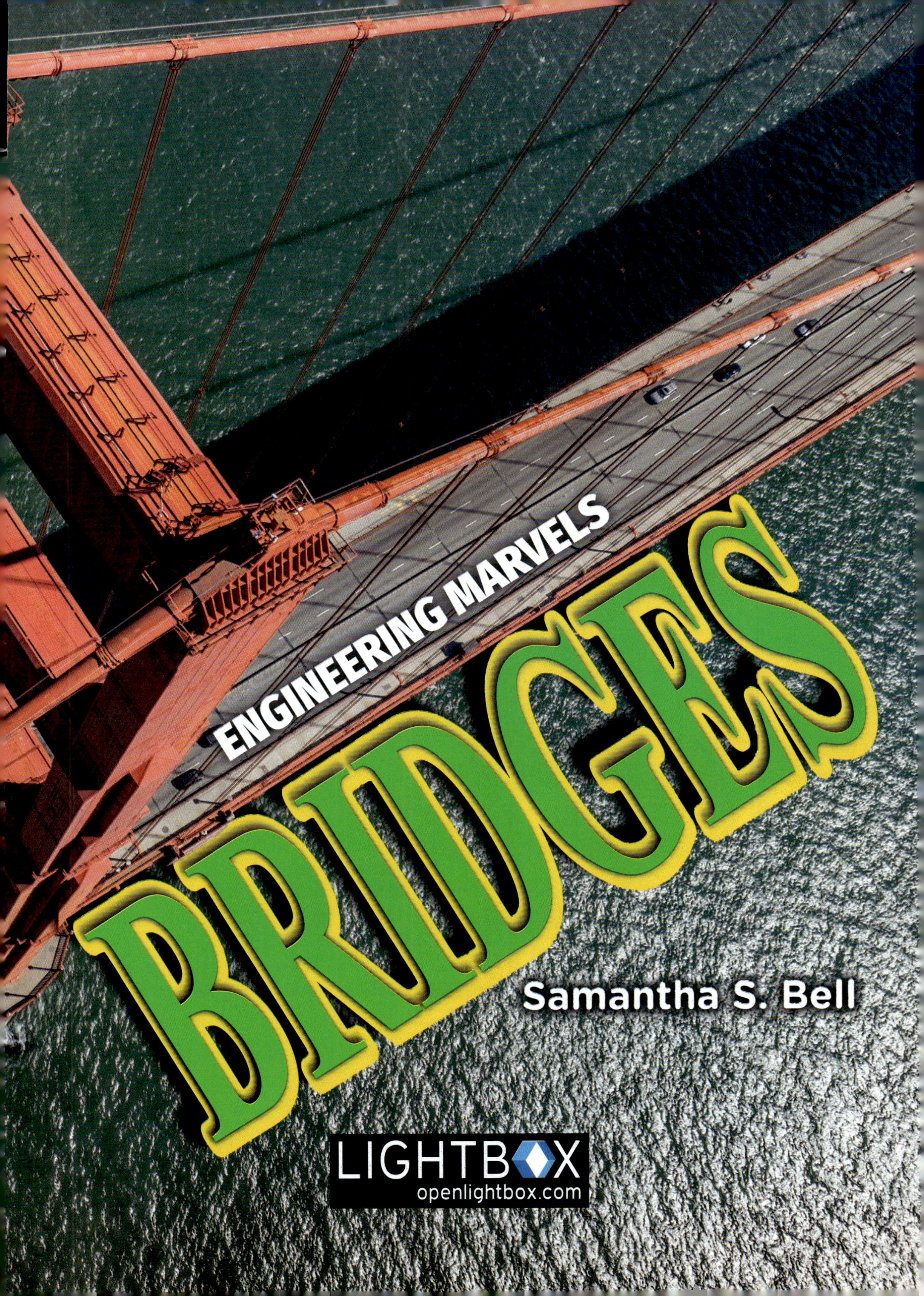

ENGINEERING MARVELS

BRIDGES

Samantha S. Bell

LIGHTBOX
openlightbox.com

LIGHTBOX

Go to
www.openlightbox.com
and enter this book's
unique code.

ACCESS CODE

LBA96898

Lightbox is an all-inclusive digital solution for the teaching and learning of curriculum topics in an original, groundbreaking way. Lightbox is based on National Curriculum Standards.

STANDARD FEATURES OF LIGHTBOX

AUDIO High-quality narration using text-to-speech system

ACTIVITIES Printable PDFs that can be emailed and graded

SLIDESHOWS Pictorial overviews of key concepts

VIDEOS Embedded high-definition video clips

WEBLINKS Curated links to external, child-safe resources

TRANSPARENCIES Step-by-step layering of maps, diagrams, charts, and timelines

INTERACTIVE MAPS Interactive maps and aerial satellite imagery

QUIZZES Ten multiple choice questions that are automatically graded and emailed for teacher assessment

KEY WORDS Matching key concepts to their definitions

Contents

Chapter 1

Crossing and Connecting

Twelve-year-old Jin stands in line with his family. He is waiting for his turn to walk across the Zhangjiajie Grand Canyon Glass Bridge in China. The bridge is made of 99 glass panels. Each has three layers and can support 40 tons (36 metric tons). Finally, it's Jin's turn to cross the amazing 1,400-foot (430-meter) bridge.

About 700 tourists can be on the Zhangjiajie Grand Canyon Glass Bridge at any one time.

Jin watches as some visitors hold the railings. Others crawl on their hands and knees. But Jin walks bravely across. He can see the 1,000-foot (300-m) drop beneath his feet.

Bridges are structures people use to get across a river, road, or other obstacle. A bridge can be a simple piece of rope. Or it can be a complex structure of towers and cables.

The ancient Romans were among the first to show their skills in bridge building. Their bridges had arches made of stone. But they needed to make the bridges stronger and sturdier. By 2 BCE, they had discovered how to make waterproof **concrete**. Using a **cofferdam**, they could make a concrete bridge.

The ancient Chinese also built bridges. They used wood, stone, bamboo, and iron chain.

The Romans built a stone bridge in Cordoba, Spain, in the first century CE.

The ancient **Romans** built more than **1,000 stone bridges** in Europe, Africa, and Asia.

The **oldest bridge** in the world still in use is in **Turkey**. It is from **850 BCE**.

The people of Cherrapunji, India, **build bridges** by twisting the living roots of **trees**. Some of these bridges are **500 years old**.

The span is the part of the bridge between supports. The span of the Tower Bridge in London, England, is 270 feet (82.3 m) long.

Bridge design did not change much until the 1100s. At that time, the Catholic Church saw the importance of good roads for communication. That meant more bridges were needed. Priests worked to design and construct them.

Traders also needed bridges. They traveled from city to city with their goods. As the centuries passed, bridge builders introduced new types of materials. These materials led to new building methods. Bridge construction became more scientific than ever before.

Engineers are still designing, building, and improving bridges today. These structures do more than just cross an **expanse**. Some help inspire emotions, such as awe or wonder. Others **commemorate** significant events. But they all are a way to connect people with their communities.

Chapter 2

Strong Designs, Strong Bridges

Architects and engineers work to design bridges that are functional, safe, and often beautiful. One of the first things they consider is the dead load. This is the weight of the structure itself. Next, they consider the live load. This is the people and objects that will cross the bridge.

Engineers plan for other factors as well. For example, they plan for natural events such as ice, wind, or earthquakes. They also consider what might happen on the bridge, such as vehicles hitting the bridge.

The Bay Bridge's towers rest 526 feet (160 m) above the waters of the San Francisco Bay in California.

Next, they must choose the best materials to use. The bridge needs to be strong enough to carry all of the loads that will travel on the bridge. But in most cases, the planners have a budget. As a result, the materials cannot be too expensive. Bridges can be built of stone, iron, wood, aluminum, or even plastic. However, many modern bridges are made of steel or concrete.

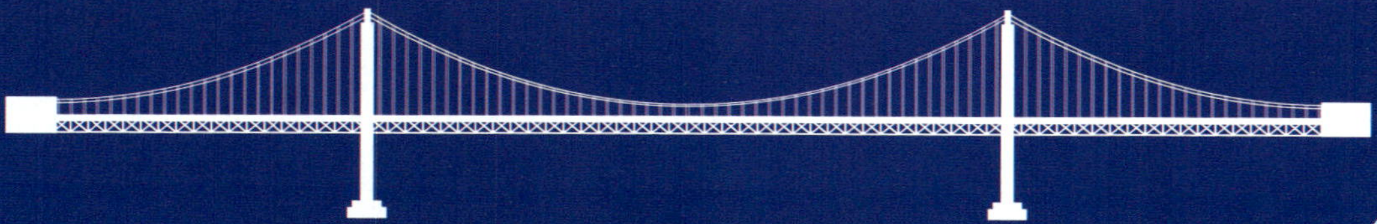

The world's **longest** bridge stretches **102.4 miles** (165 kilometers) across China.

The city of **Hamburg, Germany**, is home to an estimated **2,300 bridges**.

At least **100 million** vehicles cross the **George Washington Bridge** in New York City every year. It is the world's **busiest bridge**.

Engineers also consider the forces that will act on the bridge. Tension pulls things apart. Compression pushes things together. If there is too much of either, the material will not be able to carry the loads. That could cause the bridge to fail.

The Sydney Harbour Bridge in Australia was built using 58,400 tons (53,000 metric tons) of steel.

Different bridge designs handle these forces in different ways.

A beam bridge is one of the simplest designs. These bridges usually have at least two horizontal beams supported by **substructures**. The beams carry the loads into the substructures.

Truss bridges are made from a framework of smaller elements. These elements are often built in a triangular pattern. The triangles distribute the stress throughout the structure. They carry the load through tension or compression.

Arch bridges get their strength from their semicircle shape. This shape carries compression from the top of the arch down to the supports in the ground.

People started building arch bridges 3,000 years ago.

Suspension bridges are used for the longest spans. These bridges have high towers with two main cables. The cables extend from the land, over the towers, and back to the land on the other side. Smaller cables hang from the main cables and attach to the **deck**. The deck is held up by the cables. **Cable-stayed bridges** are another kind of suspension bridge.

The Capilano Suspension Bridge rests 230 feet (70 m) above the Capilano River in British Columbia.

Engineering Design Process

Engineers must be confident in their plans. They use various tools and do many tests in their planning. By following the engineering design process, the bridge should be strong enough for the loads.

ASK What needs to be crossed? Who or what will be crossing it? What natural factors might affect the bridge? What materials are available?

IMAGINE Brainstorm possible bridge designs. What type of bridge would work best?

PLAN Draw a diagram or create a model of the bridge. Make a list of materials needed. Write down the steps that will need to be taken to build it.

CREATE Follow the plan and build a bridge.

IMPROVE What worked with the bridge? What could be made better? How could the design change to make the bridge stronger?

Chapter 3

Galloping Gertie

Sometimes engineers make mistakes. The Tacoma Narrows Bridge was the first to cross the Puget Sound in Washington. But to keep costs down, the designer made the bridge narrower and more flexible than normal. Other engineers noticed that wind caused the bridge's deck to have wave motions.

The bridges over the Tacoma Narrows strait cut down some people's travel time by two hours.

They tried to take the bounce out by using **hydraulic jacks** as shock absorbers. However, nothing worked. The bridge became known as Galloping Gertie.

An average of 90,000 vehicles cross the Tacoma Narrows Bridge every day.

Even as Gertie opened in July 1940, engineers were trying to fix it. The next step was to add wind **deflectors**. But the engineers were too late. On November 7, steady winds blew. The deck moved up and down in waves up to 5 feet (1.5 m) high. Then a cable slipped, and Gertie began to twist. The motions became larger and larger. Within minutes, the roadway was tilting up to 28 feet (8.5 m) high. In a little more than an hour, the bridge broke apart and fell into the water.

Fortunately, people who had been on the bridge were safe. A replacement bridge was completed in 1950. It was called Sturdy Gertie. The new design included wind grates and hydraulic shock absorbers. This time, trusses were used to stiffen the bridge. In 2007, a second bridge was added to help with traffic.

Chapter 4

The Pearl Bridge in Japan is wide enough for six lanes of traffic.

The Pearl Bridge

In 1998, the Akashi Kaikyo Bridge in Japan became the world's longest suspension bridge. Its span is nearly 1.24 miles (2 km) long. The structure is known as the Pearl Bridge. More than 1,000 lights are attached to its cables. At night, they look like a string of pearls.

Engineers designing the bridge faced natural challenges. The bridge was built in water 360 feet (110 m) deep. The ground under the bridge could experience an earthquake. Meanwhile, winds could reach speeds up to 179 miles per hour (288 km/h). To be sure the design worked, researchers built the world's largest wind tunnel facility to test it. In total, construction of the bridge took 10 years.

Mapping Bridges

Some of the most best-known bridges in the world can be found in the United States. The map shows where a few of these engineering marvels are located. Are there any large bridges near where you live?

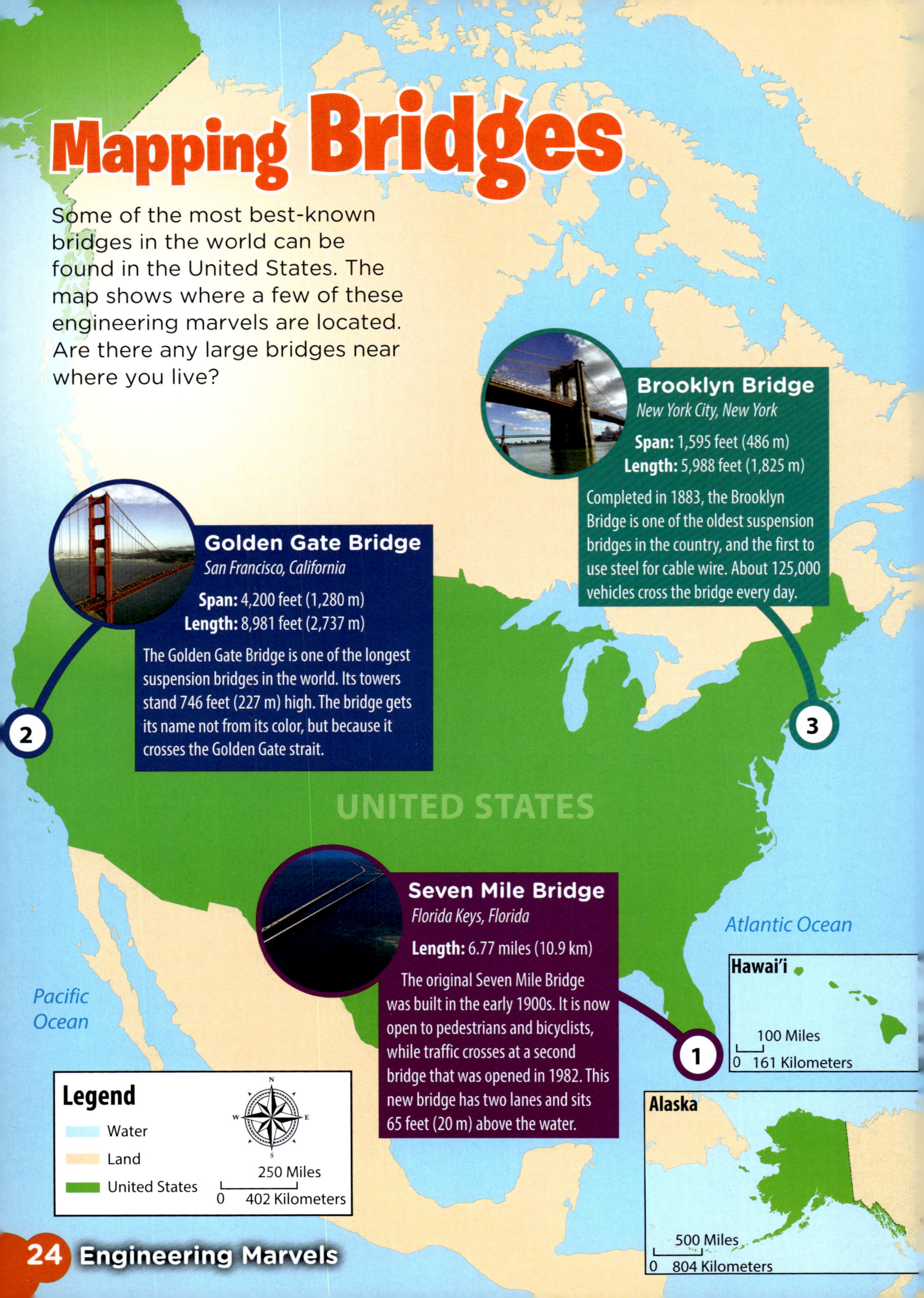

Brooklyn Bridge

New York City, New York

Span: 1,595 feet (486 m)
Length: 5,988 feet (1,825 m)

Completed in 1883, the Brooklyn Bridge is one of the oldest suspension bridges in the country, and the first to use steel for cable wire. About 125,000 vehicles cross the bridge every day.

Golden Gate Bridge

San Francisco, California

Span: 4,200 feet (1,280 m)
Length: 8,981 feet (2,737 m)

The Golden Gate Bridge is one of the longest suspension bridges in the world. Its towers stand 746 feet (227 m) high. The bridge gets its name not from its color, but because it crosses the Golden Gate strait.

Seven Mile Bridge

Florida Keys, Florida

Length: 6.77 miles (10.9 km)

The original Seven Mile Bridge was built in the early 1900s. It is now open to pedestrians and bicyclists, while traffic crosses at a second bridge that was opened in 1982. This new bridge has two lanes and sits 65 feet (20 m) above the water.

Timeline

Today, bridges span thousands of waterways in the United States. Millions of people cross them every day in vehicles, on bikes, or on foot. Discover more about the history of bridges in the United States.

1697

The oldest U.S. bridge still in use is built in Holmesburg, Pennsylvania. The bridge was expanded in 1893 and now has a main span of 73 feet (22 m).

1839

The first iron bridge in the United States is built in Brownsville, Pennsylvania. Once only crossed by coaches and wagons, the bridge is still being used today.

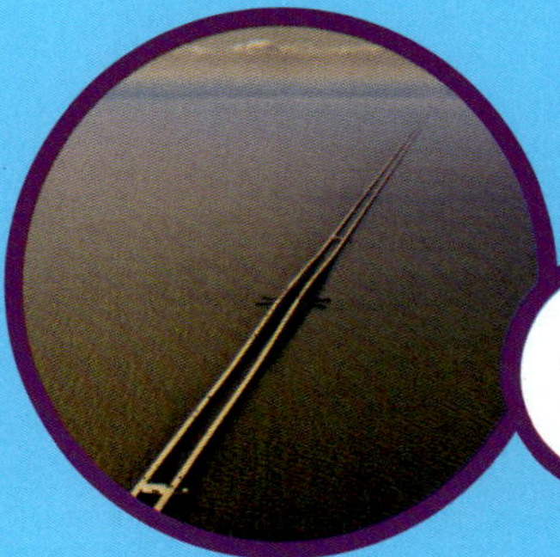

1956

The first span of Louisiana's Lake Pontchartrain **Causeway** opens to the public. The second span opens 13 years later. Totaling 24 miles (39 km) long, it is the longest bridge over water in the world.

1996

California announces plans to replace parts of the Bay Bridge. The project ends up costing $6.5 billion. It is now considered the most expensive bridge in the world.

2014

The Chesapeake Bay Bridge-Tunnel in Virginia raises its toll to $15 one-way for a passenger vehicle, making it the most expensive bridge crossing in the country.

2016

The world's longest floating bridge opens to traffic. The Evergreen Point Floating Bridge of Washington state measures 7,708 feet (2,349 m) long.

Build a Bridge

Now it is your turn to build a bridge. Yours should hold a live load of several paper clips. It should span across two stacks of books.

Materials

For this challenge, you'll need paper (different types), books, a ruler, scissors, tape, and paper clips.

Procedure

1. Place the books in two towers approximately 8 inches (20 centimeters) apart. Place a sheet of paper on the books so it spans the space between them.

2. Test the bridge by adding one paper clip at a time to the paper. How many paper clips will it hold?

3. Try a new design. Fold one long side of the paper 2 inches (5 cm) in toward the center. Do the same with the other long side of the paper. Open your paper and place it on the books. The paper bridge now has two raised sides.

4. Test the new bridge by adding one paper clip at a time to the paper.

5. Fold a second piece of paper like the first. Stack the two papers. How many paper clips can it hold now?

6. Next, take a third sheet of paper. Fold it back and forth about five times like a fan. Place this paper on top of the books. Place a new flat sheet of paper on top of it. How many paper clips can it hold now?

Improve It!

How can you make the bridge stronger?

- Use some paper and tape to make substructures. Where could you place the substructures to add the most support?
- Try using different kinds of paper, such as notebook paper, construction paper, or card stock. Which materials work the best?

Quiz

1 When did the Romans discover how to make waterproof concrete?

2 The Catholic Church thought good roads were important for what?

3 What is one of the first things bridge architects and engineers consider?

4 What are modern bridges made of?

5 What force pulls things apart?

6 How long is the world's longest bridge?

7 What is one of the simplest bridge designs?

8 Which type of bridge is used for the longest spans?

9 Where is the world's longest suspension bridge located?

10 When was the first iron bridge in the United States built?

Answers

1. By 2 BCE **2.** Communication **3.** Dead load **4.** Steel or concrete **5.** Tension **6.** 102.4 miles (165 km) long **7.** Beam bridge **8.** Suspension **9.** Japan **10.** 1697

Key Words

cable-stayed bridges: bridges with cables that attach directly from a tower to the deck

causeway: a raised road or path

cofferdam: a temporary, watertight space used to build the foundations of a bridge

commemorate: to use as a memorial or remembrance

concrete: a strong, stone-like material made from gravel, sand, cement, and water

deck: the surface of a bridge used by people, animals, or vehicles

deflectors: devices that cause something to turn or change direction

expanse: a wide area or space

hydraulic jacks: devices that use a small amount of force to lift a heavy load

substructures: the parts of a bridge that support the span from underneath

Index

LIGHTBOX

SUPPLEMENTARY RESOURCES

Click on the plus icon ⊕ found in the bottom left corner of each spread to open additional teacher resources.

- Download and print the book's quizzes and activities
- Access curriculum correlations
- Explore additional web applications that enhance the Lightbox experience

LIGHTBOX DIGITAL TITLES
Packed full of integrated media

VIDEOS

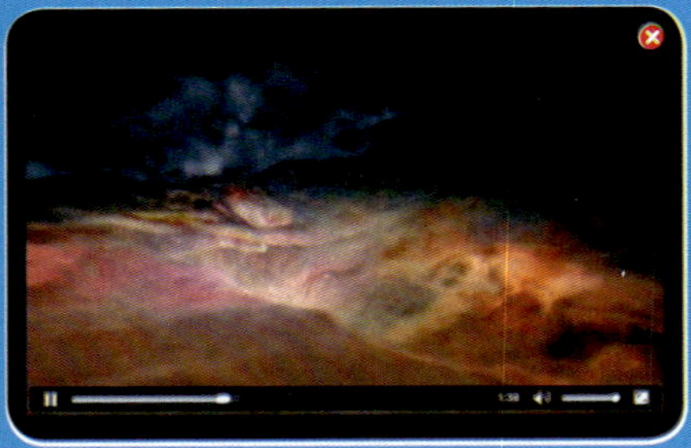

INTERACTIVE MAPS

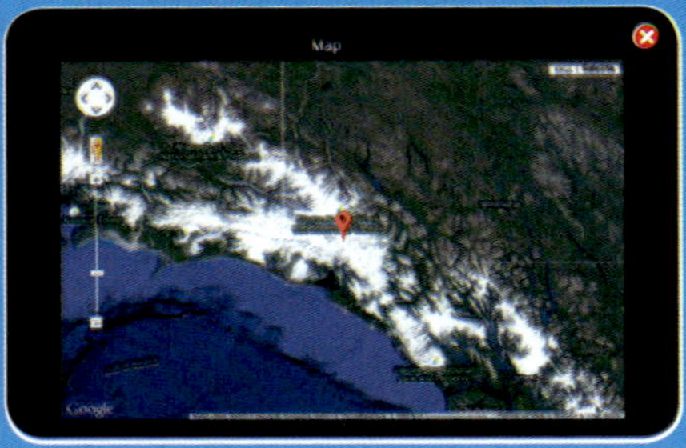

WEBLINKS

SLIDESHOWS

QUIZZES

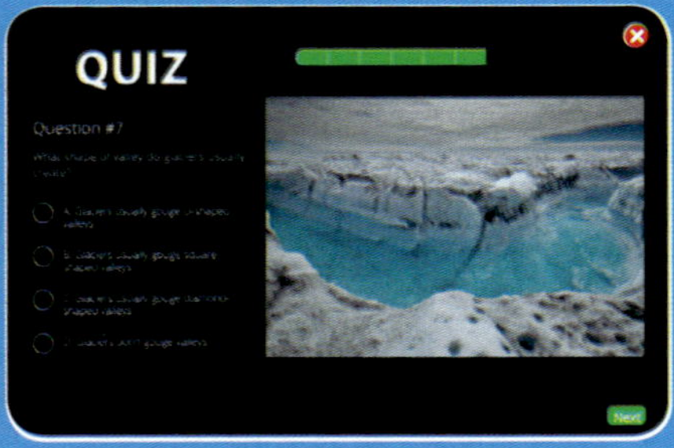

OPTIMIZED FOR

- ✔ TABLETS
- ✔ WHITEBOARDS
- ✔ COMPUTERS
- ✔ AND MUCH MORE!

Published by Smartbook Media Inc.
350 5th Avenue, 59th Floor New York, NY 10118
Website: www.openlightbox.com

012018
151217

Library of Congress Control Number: 2017961989

ISBN 978-1-5105-3745-3 (hardcover)
ISBN 978-1-5105-3746-0 (multi-user eBook)

Printed in the Brainerd, Minnesota, United States
1 2 3 4 5 6 7 8 9 0 22 21 20 19 18

First published by North Star Editions in 2018.

Project Coordinator: Jared Siemens
Designer: Ana María Vidal

The publisher acknowledges Alamy, Getty Images, iStock, and Shutterstock as the primary image suppliers for this title.